# ENGELBERT HUMPERDINCK

# Evening Prayer

(Hansel and Gretel)

Soprano, Mezzo-Soprano and Piano

Edited by / Herausgegeben von
Roger Nichols

EIGENTUM DES VERLEGERS · ALLE RECHTE VORBEHALTEN
ALL RIGHTS RESERVED

# EDITION PETERS

LONDON · FRANKFURT/M. · LEIPZIG · NEW YORK

# PREFACE

## Historical introduction

After studying at the Conservatories of Cologne and Munich, Humperdinck was invited by Wagner to Bayreuth where in 1881–2 he helped prepare for the premiere and publication of *Parsifal*. From 1890 to 1897 he was a professor at the Frankfurt Conservatory and opera critic of the *Frankfurter Zeitung*, and it was at the start of this period that his sister, Adelheid Wette, asked him to set four folksongs to include in a play of *Hansel and Gretel* to be performed by her children. His opera grew from these modest beginnings. It was premiered at the Court Theatre in Weimar on 23 December 1893, conducted by Richard Strauss who described it as "a masterpiece of the highest quality ... all of it original, new and so authentically German". The opera was a tremendous success and within a year it had been produced in over 50 theatres in Germany.[*] It was also the first opera to be broadcast complete from Covent Garden, in January 1923. Humperdinck wrote six more operas, but none of them matched the success of the first.

[*]Peter Jonas, article on *Hänsel und Gretel* in *The Viking Opera Guide*, ed. Amanda Holden with Nicholas Kenyon and Stephen Walsh (London, 1993), p. 492

## The story

The tale of Hansel and Gretel was published by Wilhelm and Jacob Grimm in 1812. Adelheid Wette toned down some of the more alarming features of this original, such as the murderous intent of the Mother, and brought in the sympathetic characters of the Father, the Sandman, the Dew Fairy and the fourteen angels.

In Act I Hansel and Gretel have annoyed their Mother by dancing when they should have been making brooms and knitting. In her anger the Mother knocks over the jug of milk, the only food in the house. She sends the children out into the nearby forest to pick strawberries, but when the Father returns he is horrified, because this is where the Witch lives in her gingerbread cottage. He and the Mother go out to find their children. In Act II, after the children have picked and then eaten the strawberries, a mist rises and, when it clears, there is the Sandman, a small grey figure with a sack on his back. He throws sand in their eyes and, after they say their evening prayer, they fall asleep in each other's arms. After the prayer, the mist descends again and turns into a magic staircase, down which come the fourteen angels of whom they sang, to surround them and keep them safe through the night.

# PRÉFACE

## Introduction historique

Après des études aux Conservatoires de Cologne et de Munich, Humperdinck est invité par Wagner à Bayreuth, où, en 1881-1882, il aide à préparer la création et la publication de *Parsifal*. De 1890 à 1897, il est professeur au Conservatoire de Francfort et critique d'opéra au *Frankfurter Zeitung*, et c'est au début de cette période que sa sœur, Adelheid Wette, lui demande de mettre en musique quatre chants populaires pour une représentation de *Hänsel und Gretel* que doivent donner ses enfants. Son opéra est né de ces modestes débuts. Il est créé au Théâtre de la cour de Weimar le 23 décembre 1893, sous la direction de Richard Strauss, qui y voit « un chef-d'œuvre du plus haut niveau […] original, nouveau et authentiquement allemand ». L'opéra est un immense succès, et en l'espace d'un an il sera donné dans plus de trente théâtres en Allemagne[*]. Ce sera également le premier opéra à être retransmis intégralement de Covent Garden, en janvier 1923. Humperdinck écrira six autres opéras, mais aucun n'égalera le succès du premier.

[*]Peter Jonas, article sur *Hänsel und Gretel* dans *The Viking Opera Guide*, éd. Amanda Holden avec Nicholas Kenyon et Stephen Walsh (Londres, 1993), p. 492.

## L'histoire

Wilhelm et Jacob Grimm publièrent le conte de Hänsel et Gretel en 1812. Adelheid Wette atténua certains des aspects les plus effrayants de l'original, telles les intentions meurtrières de la mère, et introduisit les personnages sympathiques du père, du marchand de sable, de la fée Rosée et des quatorze anges.

À l'acte I, Hänsel et Gretel ont agacé leur mère en dansant alors qu'ils auraient dû être en train de fabriquer des balais ou de tricoter. Dans sa colère, la mère renverse la cruche de lait, alors qu'il n'y a rien à manger à la maison. Elle envoie les enfants dans la forêt ramasser des fraises des bois, mais lorsque le père revient il est horrifié, car c'est là qu'habite la sorcière, dans sa maison en pain d'épices. Lui et la mère partent à la recherche de leurs enfants. À l'acte II, une fois que les enfants ont cueilli et mangé les fraises, une brume s'élève, et, lorsqu'elle se dégage, le marchand de sable apparaît – une petite figure grise avec un sac sur le dos. Il leur lance du sable dans les yeux et, après leur prière de soir, les enfants s'endorment dans les bras l'un de l'autre. Après la prière, la brume retombe et se transforme en un escalier magique, que descendent les quatorze anges qu'ils avaient invoqués, pour les entourer et les protéger pendant la nuit.

# VORWORT

## Historische Einführung

Nach Studien an den Konservatorien von Köln und München wurde Humperdinck von Wagner nach Bayreuth eingeladen, wo er 1881/82 an der Vorbereitung der Uraufführung sowie der Publikation des *Parsifal* beteiligt war. Von 1890 bis 1897 wirkte er als Professor am Konservatorium in Frankfurt und Opernkritiker der Frankfurter Zeitung, und in der ersten Phase dieser Tätigkeit bat ihn seine Schwester Adelheid Wette, vier Volkslieder für eine Bühnenfassung von *Hänsel und Gretel* zu vertonen, die ihre Kinder aufführen wollten. Aus diesen bescheidenen Anfängen erwuchs schließlich seine Oper. Sie wurde am 23. Dezember 1893 am Hoftheater Weimar uraufgeführt, und zwar unter der Leitung von Richard Strauss, der sie als "Meisterwerk erster Güte" bezeichnete und weiter dazu meinte: "...und alles originell, neu und so echt deutsch." Das Werk war ein überragender Erfolg und wurde innerhalb eines Jahres bereits an mehr als fünfzig deutschen Theatern nachgespielt.[*] Darüber hinaus war dies im Januar 1923 die erste Oper, die vollständig aus dem Opernhaus von Covent Garden im Rundfunk übertragen wurde. Humperdinck schrieb sechs weitere Opern, aber keine davon reichte an den Erfolg der ersten heran.

[*]Peter Jonas, Artikel "Hänsel und Gretel" im *Viking Opera Guide*, hg. von Amanda Holden unter Mitarbeit von Nicholas Kenyon und Stephen Walsh (London 1993), S. 492

## Die Handlung

Die Geschichte von Hänsel und Gretel wurde 1812 von Wilhelm und Jacob Grimm veröffentlicht. Adelheid Wette schwächte einige der beängstigenderen Merkmale des Originalmärchens ab, darunter die Mordabsichten der Mutter, und führte die sympathischen Figuren des Vaters, des Sandmännchens, des Taumännchens und der vierzehn Engel ein.

Im ersten Akt haben Hänsel und Gretel ihre Mutter verärgert, weil sie getanzt haben, anstatt sich wie angewiesen mit Besenbinden und Stricken zu beschäftigen. In ihrer Wut stößt die Mutter einen Topf mit Milch um, die einzige Nahrung im Hause. Sie schickt die Kinder hinaus in den nahen Wald, um Erdbeeren zu suchen, aber bei seiner Rückkehr ist der Vater darüber entsetzt, denn dort lebt die Hexe in ihrem Knusperhäuschen. Er und die Mutter machen sich auf die Suche nach ihren Kindern. Nachdem die Kinder im zweiten Akt Erdbeeren gepflückt und dann selbst gegessen haben, zieht ein Nebel herauf, und als er sich lichtet, steht vor ihnen das Sandmännchen, eine kleine graue Gestalt mit einem Sack auf der Schulter. Er streut ihnen Sand in die Augen, und nachdem sie ihr Abendgebet gesprochen haben, fallen sie eng umschlungen ein. Nach dem Gebet senkt sich der Nebel wieder herab und verwandelt sich in eine Zaubertreppe, auf der die vierzehn Engel, von denen sie zuvor gesungen haben, herabsteigen und sie umringen, um sie die Nacht hindurch zu beschützen.

# Evening Prayer
from Hänsel and Gretel

Engelbert Humperdinck
(1854–1921)

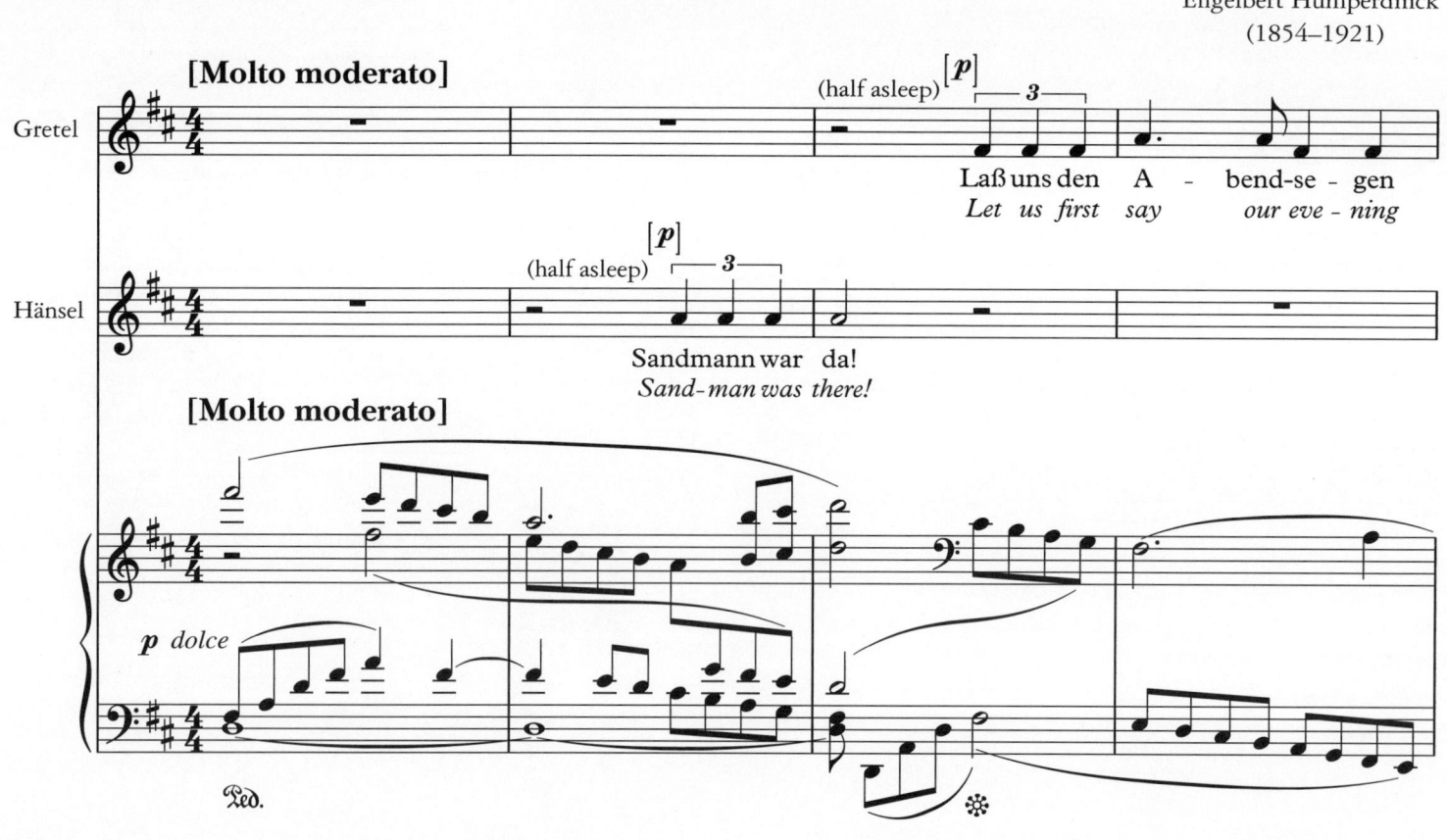

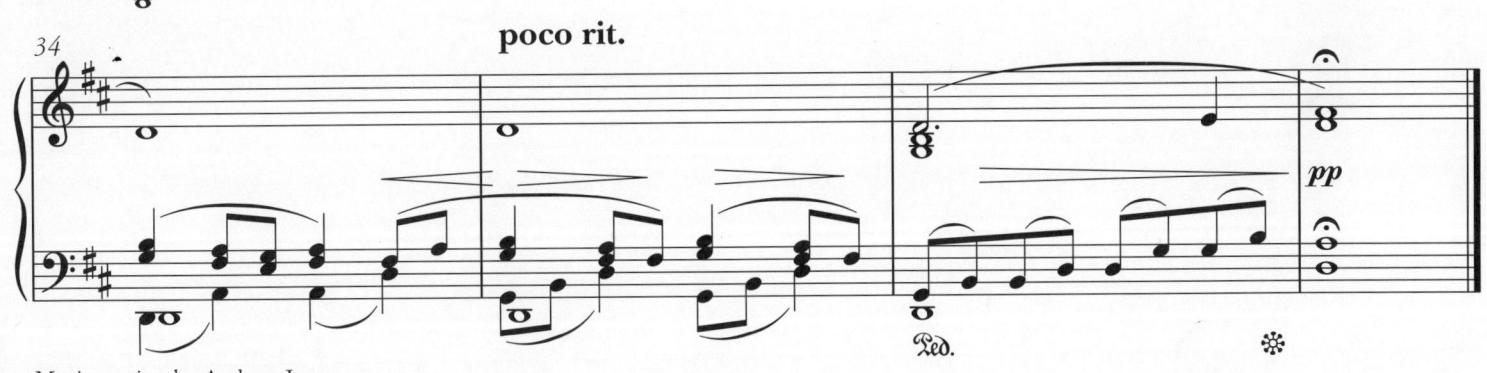

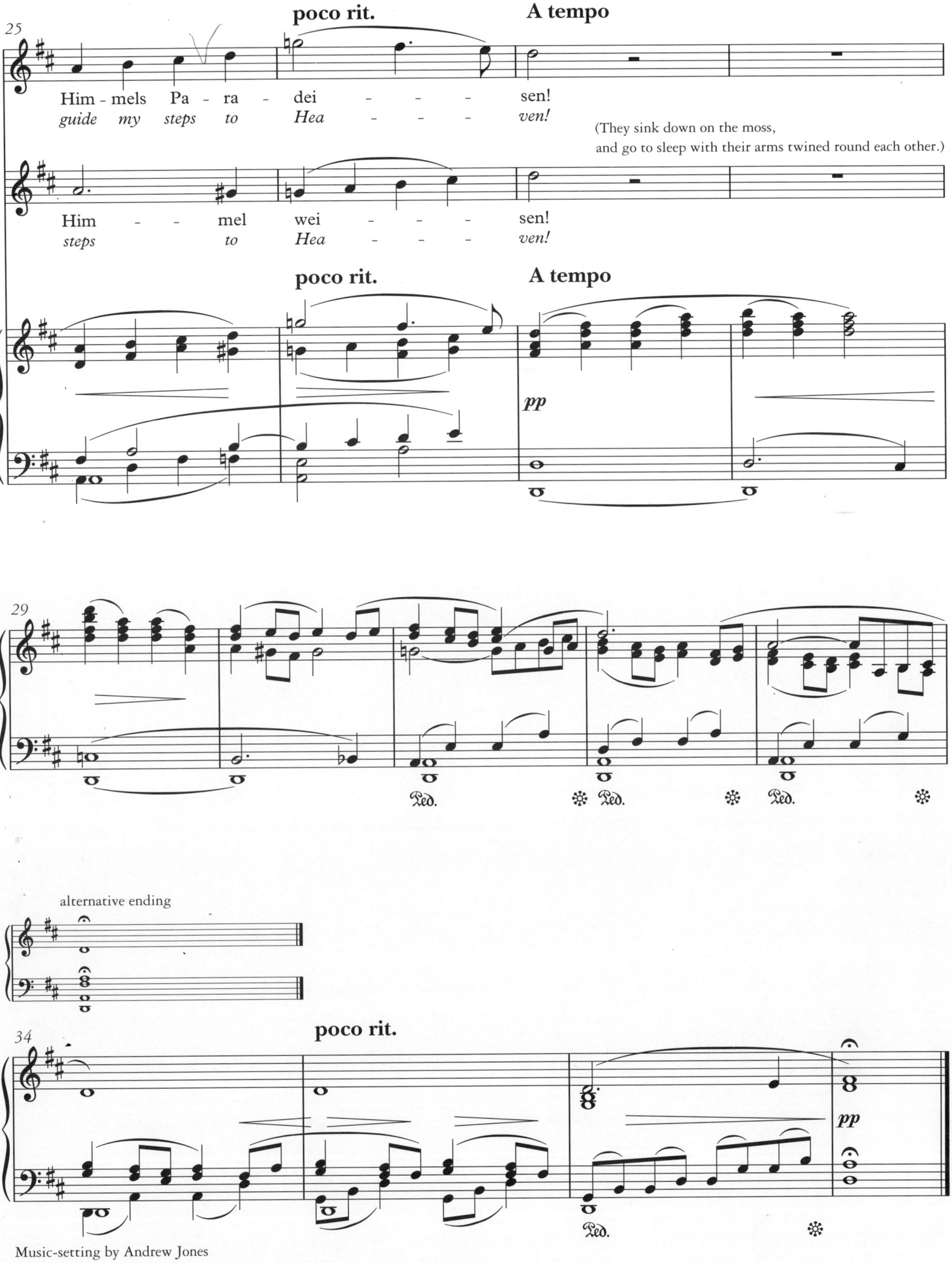


Music-setting by Andrew Jones
Printed by Caligraving Limited, Thetford, Norfolk

# CRITICAL COMMENTARY

**Sources**
Vocal score by R. Kleinmichel (Mainz, Schott, 1895; Plate no. 25788), with English words by Constance Bache

Full score (London, Eulenburg, c. 1955; Plate no. 28600)

**Editorial policy**
This edition follows in every detail the 1895 vocal score, which is entirely congruent with the full score. Constance Bache's familiar translation has been retained.
A longer run-in to the prayer is not feasible since the music leading up to the first bar of this edition derives from the Sandman's solo. Three possible endpoints can be taken: either at bar 23, where the voices end, or at one of the two other alternatives suggested.